THRESHER SHARK

GREAT

HAMMERHEAD
SHARK

BASKING SHARK

GREAT WHITE

SHARK

BLUE SHARK

To the reader—sometimes
things that look scary
deserve a closer look.
—J.M.

MARINE BIOLOGY
DEPT.

Copyright © 2022 by Jill McDonald

All rights reserved. Published in the United States by Doubleday, an imprint of
Random House Children's Books, a division of Penguin Random House LLC, New York.

Doubleday and Hello, World! are registered trademarks and the
Doubleday colophon is a trademark of Penguin Random House LLC.

Visit us on the Web! rhcbooks.com

Educators and librarians, for a variety of teaching tools, visit us at RHTeachersLibrarians.com

Library of Congress Cataloging-in-Publication Data is available upon request.
ISBN 978-0-593-56481-3 (trade) — ISBN 978-0-593-56482-0 (lib. bdg.) —
ISBN 978-0-593-56483-7 (ebook)

MANUFACTURED IN CHINA   10 9 8 7 6 5 4 3 2 1   First Edition

HELLO, WORLD!®
KIDS' GUIDES

Exploring

SHARKS

Jill McDonald

Doubleday Books for Young Readers

Sharks get a bad rap.

Are they dangerous predators or misunderstood animals that are helping our oceans?

* There are over 400 different species of sharks.

Some sharks are as long as a school bus, and some can fit in your hand. Some eat large sea animals, and others only eat small things like fish eggs and plankton.

All sharks are important to the health of Earth's oceans. From the top of the food chain, sharks help oceans stay healthy by keeping all the animal species in balance.

Humans are more dangerous to sharks than sharks are to humans, and today, many sharks are endangered.

Let's dive deep and meet some of these incredible fish.

* One name for a group of sharks is a shiver!

Big or small, all sharks have similar body parts.

Most fish have bones, but a shark's skeleton is made of light, flexible cartilage. This helps sharks float and save energy while they're swimming. Do you know what else is made of cartilage? Your nose and ears!

FIRST—
DORSAL FIN

EYE

NOSTRIL

SNOUT—

TEETH

MOUTH

GILLS

PECTORAL FIN—

Sharks don't have lungs like humans. They have gills, which take in oxygen from the water that goes into their mouth. Then the gills pump the water back out.

You have one row of teeth in your upper jaw and one row in your lower jaw. But not sharks! Sharks' teeth are in many rows, and as soon as they lose a tooth, a new one grows in.

* A shark can lose and grow thousands of teeth in its lifetime.

SECOND
DORSAL FIN

CAUDAL FIN

PELVIC
FIN

ANAL
FIN

Sharks swing their strong tail back and forth to propel them forward. Their pectoral fins are used to steer and lift them in the water.

* Sharks can be found in every ocean on Earth!

EAR

The
great white shark

is a big fish with a big bite! It's the ocean's top hunter, the largest predatory fish in the world.

SERRATED TOOTH

* Great white sharks' triangular serrated teeth dig into their prey, making it hard to escape.

This huge and strong shark is fast!

Its powerful tail drives it through the water, and its enormous size helps propel it forward, so it can sneak up quickly on its prey.

* The great white shark's dramatic leap out of the water is called a breach.

Did you know sharks have ears? It's true! They can hear their prey moving in the water. Even a tiny vibration will let them know food is nearby.

CHOMP! The great white shark's powerful jaw is a hunting machine. It can have up to 300 razor-sharp teeth at one time, in up to seven rows.

The STATS

Scientific name:
Carcharodon carcharias

Location:
Mild, tropical, and cold oceans and coasts around the world

Maximum length:
20 feet (6 m)

Maximum weight:
7,000 pounds (3,200 kg)

Color:
Gray with white belly

Top swimming speed:
35 miles per hour (56 kph)

Number of pups per litter:
2–14

Life span:
Up to 70 years

QUESTION

What's your favorite thing about the great white shark?

Meet the world's largest fish, the whale shark.

Whale sharks

are enormous! But these ocean giants are gentle, slow, and harmless, eating only small fish, shrimp, plankton, and fish eggs. (And lots of them!)

Whale sharks' mouths can be as wide as 4 feet (1.2 m), but they can't bite or chew. Instead, they suck in their food along with thousands of gallons of water at a time, like an ocean vacuum cleaner.

Sharkskin is covered in tiny, flat scales called denticles, which help sharks glide easily through the water. The whale shark's eyes are covered in these scales too, like tiny teeth. Whale sharks don't have eyelids, and their eyes bulge out of the sides of their head, so these scales act as armor.

DENTICLES

* Plankton are small creatures and plants that drift close to the surface and are food for larger marine animals.

The STATS

Scientific name:
Rhincodon typus

Location:
Warm, mild, and tropical oceans around the world

Maximum length:
66 feet (20 m)

Maximum weight:
41,000 pounds (18,600 kg)

Color: Gray with cream spots

Top swimming speed: 5 miles per hour (8 kph)

Number of pups per litter: Up to 300

Life span: Up to 130 years

QUESTION

Would you like to go diving in a shark tank to swim with sharks?

The basking shark

has a very big mouth, but it uses it to eat very small things! This huge and unusual-looking shark may seem a little scary, but it's quite gentle.

PLANKTON

Like the whale shark, the basking shark is a filter feeder. It sweeps the ocean, gulping large amounts of water into its mouth and using its gills to filter out plankton to eat.

Scientific name:
Cetorhinus maximus

Location:
Coasts of arctic and mild waters around the world

Maximum length:
40 feet (12 m)

Maximum weight:
10,000 pounds (4,500 kg)

Color:
Dark gray, darker on the top and lighter underneath

Top swimming speed:
4 miles per hour (6 kph)

Number of pups per litter:
Up to 6

Life span:
Up to 50 years

Basking sharks got their name because they are slow-moving and like to bask in the sun near the surface of the water, just like when you float lazily in a pool on a warm day.

* Many years ago, sailors and fishermen would sometimes be confused by this shark's enormous mouth and think they had spotted a sea monster!

QUESTION

What would you call the basking shark if you gave it a new name?

It's easy to see how the

great hammerhead

shark got its name. With eyes
far apart on either side of
their long, rectangular head,
hammerheads might
look a little odd.

But the shape of their head gives them an advantage:
Their far-apart eyes get a full view of what's
around them. They can even use their head to
pin down prey, such as stingrays.

* There are ten different species of hammerhead shark. The great hammerhead is the largest.

Hammerheads have pores on their head that act like sensors. They help them find their way, alert them to changes in temperature, and detect signals coming from their prey.

Hammerhead sharks are in danger of extinction from overfishing and being caught in fishing nets. They are listed as critically endangered by the International Union for Conservation of Nature.

The STATS

Scientific name:
Sphyrna mokarran

Location:
Warm and tropical oceans and coastlines worldwide

Maximum length:
20 feet (6 m)

Maximum weight:
1,000 pounds (450 kg)

Color:
Brownish gray on top, cream underneath

Top swimming speed:
25 miles per hour (40 kph)

Number of pups per litter:
6–42

Life span:
Up to 44 years

QUESTION

What ways can you think of to help protect sharks?

Look at the amazing tail fin of the

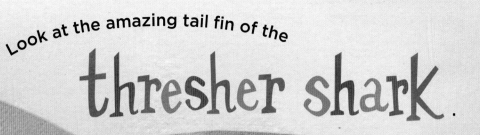

thresher shark.

This shark is harmless to humans and even a bit shy. But when it's time for a meal, the thresher shark uses its long, powerful tail fin to whip and stun smaller fish.

On some thresher sharks, the tail fin is as long as the shark's body!

There are three species of thresher shark: pelagic, bigeye, and common thresher. But experts believe there may be a fourth species they haven't found yet! Even scientists are always learning.

* Most sharks are cold-blooded, but not the thresher shark. It has warm blood, like you do. This keeps the thresher's muscles warm and helps it swim faster.

* The thresher shark shares its name with a piece of farm equipment. A thresher is a machine that beats grain to remove the seeds from the stalk.

The STATS

Scientific name:
Alopias vulpinus

Location:
Tropical, mild, and cold oceans and coasts worldwide

Maximum length:
25 feet (7.5 m)

Maximum weight:
750 pounds (340 kg)

Color:
Brownish gray or black on top, white or light gray underneath

Top swimming speed:
30 miles per hour (48 kph)

Number of pups per litter:
2

Life span:
Up to 50 years

QUESTION

If you were a shark, what kind of tail would you want?

Not all sharks are huge with big, meat-eating jaws. Some sharks are mini!
The world's smallest shark doesn't grow any longer than 8 inches (20 cm).

The dwarf lantern lives off the coasts of Colombia and Venezuela. This tiny shark is bioluminescent, which means it can glow!

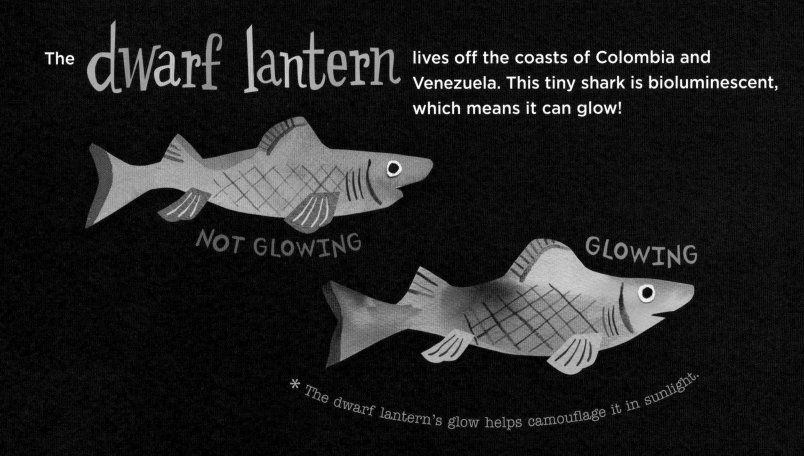

NOT GLOWING

GLOWING

* The dwarf lantern's glow helps camouflage it in sunlight.

You probably won't ever see a

Pale catshark,

and not just because it's small.
Scientists have only found this shark once!
It measured just over 8 inches long (20 cm).

Green lanternsharks

are just 10 inches (25 cm) long. But being small doesn't stop them from attacking prey larger than themselves, such as squid and octopuses!

* Despite its name, this shark is not green.

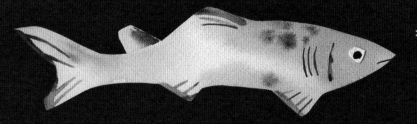

Here's a mini shark with a sweet name: the # lollipop catshark.

It has a round head and a skinny body, like a large tadpole. This tiny shark is very soft and squishy. The longest one ever found was 11 inches (28 cm).

The panama ghost catshark

can grow to 9 inches (23 cm). This tiny shark does most of its hunting at night, finding food on the ocean floor.

Shark babies are called PUPS.
They can be born in three different ways,
depending on the type of shark.

Some sharks have live births. The baby grows inside its
mother's body until it's ready to be born—just like you did!

Other shark mothers lay eggs, which have a tough,
leathery case to keep the shark embryos safe. The mother
hides the eggs in a reef or the seabed until they hatch.

Shark egg cases have different shapes.
Some look like a flat beetle.
Others are spiral-shaped.

Some sharks hold their eggs inside
them, to protect them from predators.
The eggs will hatch inside the mother
when the pups are ready to be born.

SHARK
EGGS

The **blue shark** can give birth to as many as 135 live shark pups at one time.

* Shark pups can swim and hunt as soon as they are born.
Shark mothers do not need to look after their babies.

Sand tiger sharks

only have two pups, every two years.

* Great white shark pups are 5 feet (1.5 m) long at birth!
That's the size of the average park bench.

We know that some sharks eat other fish, but did you know they can also be friends?

The pilot fish and the whitetip shark help each other. The pilot fish swims into the shark's mouth to pick out bits of food to eat. In return, the shark gets its teeth cleaned!

whitetip shark

PILOT FISH

It's rare for a whitetip shark to eat a pilot fish, as both animals need each other to stay healthy.

* Groups of pilot fish are loyal to their shark and stay with it, even chasing other pilot fish away from their buddy.

Remora fish stick to their friends—literally!
The remora has a suction cup on its head that allows it
to stick to a shark. It eats parasites off the shark's skin,
so the remora gets a meal and the shark gets cleaned up!

* This relationship is called
  mutualism—where both fish
  benefit from one another.

suction cup

REMORA FISH

Sharks have lived on Earth for over 450 million years. Let's go way back in time and swim with the distant relatives of today's sharks.

If you think whale sharks are big, say hello to

Megalodon,

the largest shark ever. Megalodon lived over 20 million years ago and grew to lengths of 60 feet (18 m), about as long as a bowling lane! Scientists have found fossilized Megalodon teeth that are 7 inches (18 cm) long. That's about the length of a pencil!

Over 300 million years ago, a shark with a jaw like a pair of scissors swam the oceans.

The teeth of # Edestus

weren't in a curved jaw, as on today's sharks. Instead, this shark cousin had a jaw that stuck out from its mouth, with vertical lines of razor-sharp teeth that slashed at its prey.

Xenacanthus

is also known as an eel shark. This slim shark, which had a long spike sticking out of its head, existed until 200 million years ago. Scientists think its spike might have been venomous, like a stingray's tail spine.

Stethacanthus

was a small shark, at about 3 feet (1 m) long, but this 300-million-year-old shark cousin had a very unusual feature: a fin shaped like an ironing board! Its strange shape likely made it a slower swimmer, but scientists think the fin might have been useful in scaring off predators and attracting mates.

How would you like to work
with sharks one day?
You can!

Marine biologists are scientists who study ocean life.
They share the information they find so we can better
understand what lives underwater. Shark researchers
can attach tags to sharks that allow them to follow
and study their movements.

Scuba divers can be part of a scientific crew, and
can also take tourists to see sharks from the safety of an
underwater cage. By sharing their love of sharks, divers help
us understand how important it is to keep sharks safe.

* "Scuba" stands for "**s**elf-**c**ontained
underwater **b**reathing **a**pparatus."

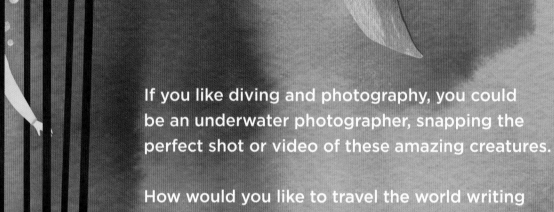

If you like diving and photography, you could be an underwater photographer, snapping the perfect shot or video of these amazing creatures.

How would you like to travel the world writing about sharks? You could be a science journalist, researching sharks and the environment and writing articles to keep everyone informed.

There are lots of ways to study and help sharks.

Which one would you choose?